# EmojiCARDS
## Activity Guide

Paradigm Shift

Ryan Eller & Jerrod Murr

# Table of Contents

# EmojiCARDS
# Activity Guide

## What areEmojiCARDS?

EmojiCARDS were created for educators, counselors, group leaders, and all individuals who need a creative way to explain emotions to their group.

These cards invite participants to engage in conversation about their emotions, feelings, or experiences. Leaders can use these cards in a multitude of ways – as a processing tool, an icebreaker, leadership initiative, or for just plain fun.

The activities in this book take full advantage of the fun, yet powerful emotions that are displayed on EmojiCARDS. Group leaders of all skill levels and experiences can use EmojiCARDS to promote two separate areas of learning…discovering emotions and processing emotions.

# How to Use this Book

## The User Guide

There are 36 different EmojiCARDS in each pack. The emotions on each card range from ridiculously happy to frustratingly mad. Cards also represent love, anxiety, apathy, and chagrin.

EmojiCARDS were created to help individuals and groups express their emotions through a visual aid. The EmojiCARDS are intentionally not labeled so each participant can use their perception to associate the card to a certain emotion.

Activities in this book are listed alphabetically and provide simple sections that help you better understand how to discover and process emotions through each activity.

### Group Size
The ideal size of the group for the activity.

### Time
The recommend amount of time to lead the activity (times are approximate and can be changed to fit the needs of your group).

### Objective
Brief description that explains the goals of activity. Continue reading to get a better understanding of how to use the EmojiCARDS.

## Discovering Emotions

This is the "How-To" section of the activity. It includes any relevant information that would be helpful before introducing the activity and step-by-step instructions for the actual facilitation of the activity.

## Processing Emotions

Recommendations for ending the activity and processing questions to discuss the activity's relevance. Some activities focus heavily on the processing portion of EmojiCARDS.

## Questions to Ask

At the end of each activity, we have suggested a handful of questions to help your participants discover and process their emotions. Questions are not mandatory for a successful activity, and these are not the only questions you can ask your group. We encourage you to ask questions that are customized to your group.

## Variations

We invite you to add your own flair and experience while using EmojiCARDS. These activities are merely a framework on how to use the cards. What makes EmojiCARDS special is when the group facilitator uses creativity to best fit the needs of the participants. We have added a few variations to each activity that you can use to mix things up.

# Check In

## Objective:

Use EmojiCARDS for a quick Check In at the beginning of an activity, day, or event to gauge the emotional state of a group.

## Discovering Emotions:

1.  Spread the EmojiCARDS face up on a table, floor, or surface so that all of the participants can view the different emotions.

2.  Invite the participants to pick one (or more) of the EmojiCARDS that best represents their current emotional state.

3.  Encourage the participants to share the reason they picked their card in the manner you find most appropriate for your group…either in pairs or as a large group.

## Processing Emotions:

Check Ins are particularly effective at the beginning of a day. This will allow participants to better understand not just their emotions, but the emotions of the group.

*(Let's Check-In now! Are you enjoying this book so far?)*

1

# Check In

## Questions to Ask:

1. What has already happened today that caused you to pick your card?

2. Do you want to keep that emotion for today? Would you rather have a different card (See Expectations on pg. 13)

3. How can you improve your mood or maintain your positive emotion?

4. Did anyone in the group pick a card that surprised you?

## Variations:

**Check In Within a Check In.** Use a Check In during the middle of a strenuous meeting or day to check the mood of the group. You can also use this after an activity. The difference between a Check In and EmojiCARDS Processing is mostly the length of the activity. Check Ins are typically quick and provide framework for the group's next actions.

*(I am as cool as the other side of the pillow)*

# Commonalities

## Objective:

This activity helps participants find connections within a group, and how those connections affect everyday life.

## Discovering Emotions:

1. Give each participant a card, and invite them to investigate the commonalities their card may have with other cards.

2. It may be easy to find simple connections, such as color, smiles, etc.,, but encourage creativity within the commonalities and give bonus points to the most creative commonality.

3. When the groups form, invite them to share their card's connection and then to discuss what connections they may have as individuals.

## Processing Emotions:

Often when determining commonalities, participants can find it hard to fit in with the small groups that begin to form. Ask the participants if they have ever been in that situation. Use the questions on the next page as guidelines to help understand social norms.

*(You're awesome! I'd connect with you any day!)*

# Commonalities

## Questions to Ask:

1.  If you are on the outside looking in, what did it feel like to be left out?

2.  If you are in a group and see someone looking to connect, what can you do to include them into your group?

3.  What ways did you connect with others?

4.  Was it easier to find commonalities with people you knew well or people you didn't know as well?

## Variations:

**Commonalities Part 2.** Encourage the participants to create Commonalities again. This time, however, ask them to find connections with other cards who were not in their original group. Invite them to find commonalities with their new group. See if that was harder to do.

**Group Commonalities.** Ask them to connect again, with different cards they haven't connected with yet. Challenge them to find connections that are deeper than the previous round. Each round gets more and more challenging but encourages participants to find deeper connections.

*(I love you. Can we make a connection?)*

# Describe Yourself

## Objective:

Individuals can often have trouble introducing themselves to a group. There is power in using a visual guide (in this case, an EmojiCARD) to express yourself.

## Discovering Emotions:

1. Spread the EmojiCARDS face up on a table, floor, or surface so that all of the participants can view the different emotions.

2. Invite the participants to find an EmojiCARD that best fits their personality.

3. Next, encourage the participants to describe their personality to the group while using their card as a visual representation.

## Processing Emotions:

Remember to encourage participants to share in the manner which best suits your group. It is important to not put the person sharing on the spot! Go first and set the stage for the rest of the group.

*(Who am I?)*

# Describe Yourself

## Questions to Ask:

1. What is your favorite food, movie, music, or place to visit and how do those things impact you?

2. Do you feel like others see you differently than you see yourself?

3. How would someone close to you describe you?

4. How do you think people who don't know you very well describe you?

5. In what ways does your personality really show?

## Variations:

**Describe Someone Else.** Pick the EmojiCARD that best describes someone close to you (mom, dad, best friend, etc.).

**Describe Me.** Pick the EmojiCARD that others would describe you with. Pick one that your mentors, teachers, leaders, or boss would choose.

*(Is it hot in here? I'm not sweating, right?)*

# EmojiCARDS Chart

*GROUP SIZE: 1-36*          *TIME: 5 MIN*

## Objective:

Teachers or leaders who work with a group that meets often can create an EmojiCARDS Chart that participants use to display their emotions on that particular day.

## Discovering Emotions:

1. Create a chart that has all of the names of the group members in a single column. Next to the column, leave a blank space where the participants will place their EmojiCARD.

2. Each day the group meets, invite the participants to grab an EmojiCARD that expresses their current emotion and place it next to their name on the chart.

3. As a group, review the chart and discuss the different emotions that are on display.

## Processing Emotions:

The EmojiCARDS Chart is a daily Check-In for groups that meet regularly and sets the tone for the day.

*(I woke up on the wrong side of the bed this morning.)*

# EmojiCARDS Chart

## Questions to Ask:

1. How does today differ from yesterday?

2. Is your current mood different than the mood you want to have? What things can we do to help you get to that emotion?

3. Do you find yourself having the same emotion every day?

4. Does your daily emotion alter how others view you?

5. What caused this emotion today?

## Variations:

**Chart Check In.** Feel free to allow the participants to change their card on the chart at any point throughout the day. Create an environment where the group can share their emotions as they express them.

**Expectations Chart.** Mix this activity with Expectations (pg. 13) and encourage the participants to share their expected outcome for the day.

*(That is an awesome chart. You are a chart machine!)*

# EmojiCARDS Processing

*GROUP SIZE: 11-36*　　　*TIME: 20 MIN*

## Objective:

Invite the participants to pick a card that best describes the emotion they are displaying after an activity or event. Basically, use EmojiCARDS to answer the question: How did it make you feel?

## Discovering Emotions:

1. Spread the EmojiCARDS face up on a table, floor, or surface so that all of the participants can view the different emotions..

2. Invite the participants to pick one (or more) of the EmojiCARDS that explains how they felt during an activity.

3. Ask processing questions to better understand the reason the participant picked their EmojiCARD.

## Processing Emotions:

It is important to know that the questions you ask fit the needs of your group. Start by asking participants questions that help them understand what happened, then why it happened, and finish by asking how it affects their life and what changes (if any) they need to make.

*(What is greater that a good processing activity? THIS book!)*

## Processing Emotions

This is the simple version of most of the activities in this book. It is the baseline of how to use these cards to process an activity.

Use the basic understanding of EmojiCARDS Processing to get better results in all of the activities you find here.

## Questions to Ask:

1. Why did you pick that card?

2. What caused you to feel that way?

3. If positive, what can you do to experience that emotion again?

4. If negative, what can you do to prevent that emotion from occurring again?

5. What control do you have over that emotion?

*(I am not quite sure how I feel about this.)*

# Emotion vs. Emotion

## Objective:

The group compares EmojiCARDS and decides which emotion is the greatest to have as a leader, teacher, friend, or any role the group wants to discuss.

## Discovering Emotions:

1. Place the cards in a tournament style bracket. I prefer to grab some tape and stick them to the wall for a great visual.

2. The participants will pick two cards that are side by side and discuss which emotion is best for a leader (or teacher or friend or husband...you get the point) to possess.

3. Discuss all of the EmojiCARDS until the group can come up with a winner amongst the emotions.

## Processing Emotions:

Once the group is finished with the activity, encourage them to develop ways in which they can start to show the top emotions.

*(Emotion vs Emotion? Did you have me as the leading card?)*

11

# Emotion vs. Emotion

## Questions to Ask:

1. Did you feel particularly connected to an EmojiCARD?

2. Did the emotion you wanted to move on to the next round get defeated? What did you do then?

3. Did you find yourself getting defensive? Why?

4. Were there emotions that didn't get promoted that are still valuable to possess?

5. What emotions did you display during the activity?

## Variations:

**Check In.** Emotion vs. Emotion is great at creating conversation about emotions. However, sometimes it can get heated. If that happens, treat it as an activity within an activity. Press pause on Emotion vs. Emotion and do a quick Check-In (pg. 1) to see if they are demonstrating the emotions they value.

*(You didn't pick me? You wanted me to cry?)*

# Expectations

## Objective:

How do you want the day to go? Use Expectations to invite participants to share their expectations for the day, activity, or event.

## Discovering Emotions:

1. Place the cards around the room and encourage the participants to think about how they would like the day to proceed.

2. Encourage the group to pick 2-5 cards that express the expectations they have for the day.

3. Invite the participants to share their expectations of the day to a partner or the rest of the group.

## Processing Emotions:

Defining expectations for a meeting, day, or event allows the entire group to get on the same page. If you are anticipating a tough day, allow the participants to set the expectations they want for the day. See if they can create ideas that will help them meet expectations.

*(Just finished "Great Expectations." Wasn't as good as I hoped!)*

# Expectations

## Questions to Ask:

1.  Do you think your expectations are going to be met?

2.  Do your expectations match those of the rest of the group?

3.  Does your attitude match your expectations?

4.  What can you do today to make your expectations a reality?

## Variations

**Expectations of Expectations.** Ask the group to complete the activity in the way described above. Next ask them to see if their expectations have changed after listening to the group's expectations.

**Group Expectations.** Once everyone has shared, invite the participants to determine which EmojiCARD (or EmojiCARDS) best fit the expectations of the entire group. .

**Expectation Check In.** At the end of the day, meeting, or event, reflect back to the beginning exercise of Expectations and see if the actual event matched their emotions.

*(I have no idea about what to expect! Or what this face means.)*

# Face Charades

## Objective:

A single participant takes an EmojiCARD from the top of the deck and tries to mimic the emoticon on the card. Their group then tries to guess the emotion on the card.

## Discovering Emotions:

1. Explain to the group that they are going to become world famous actors today! Lead them through a couple of face stretching activities by presenting a card and asking them to mimic that card.

2. Give all of the EmojiCARDS to one participant. They will pick a random card and quickly determine one word that will be the correct emotion for that card. Write the word on a hidden piece of paper.

3. As soon as the participant determines the correct emotion for the card, they start to act out the EmojiCARD in true charades fashion. The first person to guess the correct emotion gets the deck and starts again!

*(Crazy! Silly! Wild! Intense! Passionate! I give up, what is it?)*

# Face Charades

## Processing Emotions:

Although there is a ton of fun associated with this activity, it can also have a deeper meaning. What is it like to fake the emotions we see on the surface? Are we truly happy, or are you just pretending?

## Questions to Ask:

1. Who was the best actor amongst the group?

2. Do you ever feel like you are acting when showing a certain emotion?

3. Is it ever appropriate to fake an emotion?

4. Do you think others fake emotions?

## Variations

**Competition Charades.** Face Charades can be a competition if so desired. Much like the game Charades, split the group into two factions and have each team compete. A participant of each team will go to and verify that the other team is playing correctly.

*(This is howI look after a 10-hour game of Face Charades)*

# Full Value Contract

*GROUP SIZE: 2-20*                    *TIME: 15 MIN*

## Objective:

Full Value Contracts help groups create and agree upon behavioral norms. These standards help the group work successfully in the future.

## Discovering Emotions:

1.  Encourage the group to circle up for discussion and place the EmojiCARDS face up in the center of the circle.

2.  Invite the participants to think about what behaviors, emotions, and attitudes will be essential for the group to display in order to accomplish their goals.

3.  Allow the group to spend some time discussing their ideas before picking the three-five most important emotions that will represent the groups' Full Value Contract.

## Processing Emotions:

Full Value Contracts help set the stage for the rest of the group's time together. Truly invite the participants to think about their goals and expectations and what emotions will need to be shown throughout the day to achieve their goals.

*(This is the face I make when I eat too much candy!)*

# Full Value Contract

## Questions to Ask:

1. What emotions does this group need to display to work together effectively?

2. Do you agree with the EmojiCARDS chosen for the Full Value Contract?

3. Do you need a different Full Value Contract for different activities? Which ones would you choose differently?

4. How does your emotion match the Full Value Agreement of the group?

## Variations

**FVC Check In.** Display the cards chosen for the Full Value Contract for the group to see throughout the day. Encourage the participants to Check In (pg. 1) with the Full Value Contract to see if they are exhibiting the behaviors they agreed upon.

**Share and Pair.** (pg. 32). Start by asking each individual to pick a card as a FVC. Ask them to pair up and share (Pair & Share pg. 31). Encourage those pairs to create a FVC between the two. Partner with another pair and come up with a new FVC for the four. Keep going until the entire group has created a FVC.

*(Would you like to buy a car? I've got one real cheap.)*

# Group Emotion

*GROUP SIZE: 10-50*          *TIME: 20 MIN*

## Objective:

Hold up a random card until everyone from a team is mirroring the image. The fastest team is the champion. Repeat.

## Discovering Emotions:

1. Separate the group into several even-numbered teams. Do this in the most creative way possible.

2. Instruct the group that you will be holding a random card in the air, and the group that can get all of their members to mimic that emotion with their face will be the winner!

3. Repeat this until the group either tires out or reaches a certain number of victories. When finished mix the groups up and start again!

## Processing Emotions:

This activity encourages the group to work together to achieve a common goal. The faster you play the faster the group needs to collaborate.

*(What is that smell? Is that me? Oh, No! I think that is me.)*

# Group Emotion

## Questions to Ask:

1. How did your group work together to achieve the common goal?

2. What was more important during this activity... winning or having fun?

3. When can you know how to have fun as opposed to win?

4. What strategies did you use to complete the activity as quickly as possible?

## Variations

**Speed Rounds.** If you want to create more intensity and competition, try the activity with speed rounds. As soon as one group answers, show the next EmojiCARD. Do this as quickly as possible.

**Amoeba.** The team who is the last to form the emotions will lose a member to the team who was the first to finish. Play until one team has all of the members.

*(That Speed Round was much, much too fast.)*

# Introduce Yourself

GROUP SIZE: 2-10          TIME: 10 MIN

## Objective:

In this playful activity you pick a card with which you find some sort of connection. That card is now a proxy in which you will introduce yourself to the group.

## Discovering Emotions:

1. Scatter the EmojiCARDS around the room where participants will have easy access to observe the cards.

2. Ask the participants to find a card they have a connection with and arrange the group in a circle.

3. This activity works best for the imaginative participants, so foster a sense of creativity within the group by going first. Using your card as a proxy, introduce yourself to the group by mimicking the cards emotion.

## Processing Emotions:

Creativity and imagination is often easy to access for the young, but at some point we lose our ability to play. This activity encourages participants to reach into their child-like creativity to become a part of the group.

*(I have lost my imagination, do you know where it is?)*

# Introduce Yourself

## Questions to Ask:

1. Is it hard to play "make believe?"

2. At one point were you able to play without reservations?

3. When is it appropriate to play, and when is it appropriate to be serious?

4. How do you know when to be serious and when to play?

## Variations

**Improv.** After introducing yourself, switch cards and introduce yourself using the emotion.

*(Hi guys! Let me introduce myself.)*

# Line Ups

*GROUP SIZE: 15-36*     *TIME: 15 MIN*

## Objective:

Give each participant a card and ask them to line up in a certain order, such as happiest to angriest.

## Discovering Emotions:

1. Pass out random cards to participants.

2. Ask the participants to line up from happiest to angriest.

3. Try some of the variations on the next page to make the activity more challenging.

## Processing Emotions:

Line Ups are a great tool to encourage conversation, create competition, and develop critical thinking skills. Timing the team initiatives will help the group with goal setting and problem solving skills.

Also, use Line Ups to introduce different emotions to the group. As the participants try to line up, they also are trying to understand the emotions they see on their card.

*(I've got my eyes on you!)*

# Line Ups

## Questions to Ask:

1.  What emotion was the hardest emotion to define or mimic?

2.  Did you ever wish you had been given a different card?

3.  Did you come up with a plan or strategy to line up as quickly as possible?

## Variations

**Team Challenge.** Split the group into two teams. Have them compete to line up as fast as possible.

**No Noise.** Line up from angriest to happiest, but this time without talking.

**Make that Noise.** Line up from happiest to angriest, but this time only using the sound you think the emotion would make (if it is an EmojiCARD that is laughing, the participant would also be laughing).

**Facial Line Up.** Give each participant a random card. Ask them to conceal their card from the rest of the group. Line up from happiest to angriest only using your facial expression to mimic the emotion on your card.

*(Wait, you were going to eat that cookie? Oops.)*

# Match That Emotion

## Objective:

Facilitator picks an emotion for each card and creates a list with which the rest of the group tries to match with EmojiCARDS.

## Discovering Emotions:

1. Create a list that has a specific emotion for each individual EmojiCARD. See the list of emotions in the index to get ideas of emotions that will match the cards.

2. Ask the participants to match the EmojiCARDS to the emotion list you provided.

3. When the group has completed the task, reveal your list and see what differs.

## Processing Emotions:

This activity helps participants learn different ways to describe emotions. Often within a group, we hear the same ways to describe someone: happy, sad, angry, etc. Match That Emotion allows groups to learn variations of the common way we view emotions.

*(You think that is the correct match to that EmojiCARD?)*

# Match That Emotion

## Questions to Ask:

1. Do you agree with the leader's selection of emotions?

2. Do you agree with the group's matches for the EmojiCARDS?

3. What new emotions did you learn today?

4. Are there any synonyms you can use for the words the leader selected?

5. Do you ever find yourself needing a different word to describe your emotions?

6. What emotion do you use too frequently, but now you have a new words to describe?

## Variations

**Individual Challenge.** This activity can be done with a group, but can also be done with individuals. Give every participant their own list of emotions and see how well they match.

*(I can't believe you matched me with THAT EmojiCARD!)*

# Name That Emotion

## Objective:
As a group, pick a emotion to define each card.

## Discovering Emotions:

1.  This activity is much like "Match The Emotion," in the fact that the group is trying to define the EmojiCARDS.

2.  Place a sheet of paper or whiteboard in the room. Encourage the team to come up with a different emotion that matches each EmojiCARD. See the list in the index for a large list of different emotions.

3.  Encourage the group to come up with a consensus pick for each EmojiCARD.

## Processing Emotions:

This activity is for engaging conversation about different emotions. Throughout this process, each individual can use their resources to come up with the appropriate emotion to describe the appropriate EmojiCARD.

*(I can't even.)*

# Name That Emotion

## Questions to Ask:

1. What emotions did you learn today?

2. How do you describe different emotions?

3. Is there any emotion you learned today that best describes you?

4. Is there a reason why we should learn more definitions of common emotions?

## Variations

**Individual Challenge.** This activity can be done with a group, but can also be done with individuals. Give every participant their own chart and see what emotions they come up with.

**Share and Pair.** (pg. 32) Start by asking each individual to name the emotion of the EmojiCARDS. After, ask the participants to pair up and share (Pair & Share Pg. 31). Encourage the pairs to define the EmojiCARDS together. Keep combining groups until the entire group has selected what they think are the correct emotions with the EmojiCARDS.

*(This is as far as my mouth can open. Don't laugh at me!)*

# Opposites Attract

## Objective:

The group tries to find the EmojiCARDS that have an opposite card. How do these two emotions work together?

## Discovering Emotions:

1. Give each participant a random card, and invite them to find the person with the absolute opposite EmojiCARD.

2. Often, the participants will find the opposites quickly. Other times they will struggle to find each other. Encourage the participants to continue to search until the find the absolute opposite EmojiCARD.

3. Once they have the opposite pairing, ask them to come up with ways that the to emotions work well together.

## Processing Emotions:

Prideful and humble. Confident and shy. Opposites do attract. Often we see intense emotions in a negative light, but how do you use those emotions to create positive interactions.

*(You know what? I love you. That's not weird is it?)*

# Opposites Attract

## Questions to Ask:

1. What was your EmojiCARDS opposite emotion?

2. How do those cards work together? What strengths does your emotion have that compliments your opposite?

3. What strengths do you have?

4. How can your strengths work well with someone opposite of you?

5. Do you often try to work with people similar to you or opposite?

## Variations

**Similarities Attract.** Once you have found the opposite EmojiCARD, find the one that you have the most in common. How can you team up with others with similar strengths?

*(I am wearing that shirt. This is awkward.)*

# Pair and Share

## Objective:

Using an EmojiCARD, share an experience that made you feel like the emoticon on the card.

## Discovering Emotions:

1. Give each participant a card, and ask them to pair up with someone who has a similar size pinky finger (or any other creative way to pair up partners).

2. Encourage the partners to take turns sharing when they last felt the emotion displayed on their EmojiCARD.

3. After both participants have shared, the partners will switch EmojiCARDS and find someone new to share their stories.

## Processing Emotions:

Some participants have a hard time sharing emotions. Remind your group that they have the choice to share as much, or as little, as they would like to share with their partner. Also encourage the participants to be aware of others boundaries in the case of over-sharing.

*(Wooooooohoooooo! I had too much coffee today!)*

# Pair and Share

## Questions to Ask:

1. Who shared something that resonated with you?

2. Did you share something that was vulnerable? How did if make you feel?

3. Do you have a hard time sharing with others?

4. When is the right place to share? Do you need to have a certain level of trust with someone in order to share with them?

## Variations

**Share and Pair.** After grouping up with a partner and sharing, encourage the group of two to pair up with another pair of partners and share. Continue doubling the size of the groups until all of the participants are in one large group.

*(My mother says that I am beautiful.)*

# Say Hello!

## Objective:

Draw a card from the top of the deck and then invite participants to introduce themselves to others in the group while mimicking that emotion.

## Discovering Emotions:

1. This is a fun, creative, and engaging "get-to-know-you" activity. Hold up a card and make sure all participants can see it.

2. Once the participants have seen the card, encourage them to introduce themselves and share something with the other participants while mimicking that emotion.

3. After the participants have introduced themselves, hold up a new random EmojiCARD. Repeat.

## Processing Emotions:

Names bring a large amount of value to a group. This activity encourages participants to meet each other several times and start the process of learning each other's names.

*(Why do tears stream out of my face in a rainbow fashion?)*

33

# Say Hello!

## Questions to Ask:

1.  Did you meet anyone knew today? Can you share what you learned about them?

2.  How important is it for us to know each other's names?

3.  How do you feel when someone remembers your name?

4.  What techniques have you learned to remember other people's names?

## Variations

**Speed Rounds.** Flash a new EmojiCARD after about 15 seconds of intermingling. Continue until the group runs out of breath or falls over with laughter.

### Things To Share While Introducing Yourself:

| | |
|---|---|
| Name | Birthday |
| Best Travel Destination | Favorite Food |
| Favorite Cartoon | Best Moment in Life |
| Your Personal Best | Hometown |
| Favorite Sport | Oldest Friend |
| #1 Life Goal | Top Bucket List Item |

*(Why did you show me those puppy adoption commercials?)*

# Spectrums

## Objective:
Spectrums allows participants to show the group where they stand - literally - on an issue.

## Discovering Emotions:

1. Place the EmojiCARDS in a straight line along the floor from happiest to angriest. It may be helpful to have the group perform a Line Up (pg. 23) to save you a step.

2. Introduce scenarios to the group and invite the participants to stand next to the emotion they would exhibit in that situation. Encourage them to share with those around them why they chose to stand next to their emotion.

3. Present several different scenarios to the group and then invite the participants to provide their own scenarios.

## Processing Emotions:

Spectrums creates conversation on how people would react to different situations. It is not surprising that this can show differences of opinions and reactions. Cultivate those emotions and see how the group will respond.

*(This is what I look like after I work out.)*

35

# Spectrums

## Questions to Ask:

1. Did you have a hard time choosing an emotion?

2. Were you ever torn between two emotions after a situation?

3. How can you choose which emotion to display during a hard situation?

## Variations

Actual vs. Desired Reactions. Ask the participants to stand next to the EmojiCARD as described above. Next ask them to stand next to the EmojiCARD of their desired reaction to the situation.

**Spectrum Situations:**

1. You are in a traffic jam, how do you respond?
2. Your are in an elevator, how do you act?
3. You are about to present a speech to your class, how do you feel?
4. Your mom just left you alone with three small children, what does your face look like?
5. You just finished a hard one-hour workout, how does your body make you feel?

*(I have to give a speech? This is how I would feel.)*

# Storytelling

## Objective:

Small groups create and share stories that are inspired by the EmojiCARDS they draw from the pile.

## Discovering Emotions:

1.  The facilitator draws a card off of the top of the deck and starts the story by sharing a tall tale relating to the emotion on the EmojiCARD.

2.  After a couple sentences, the next person in the group draws a card off of the top of the deck and continues the story by sharing a tale related to the emotion on their EmojiCARD.

3.  Continue this until everyone in the group has had the opportunity to share their part of the story.

## Processing Emotions:

We use this activity as an opportunity to talk about the stories we tell with our lives. The better lives we live, the better stories we will be able to tell in the future. Storytelling encourages the participants to be a part of a larger story, and how intertwined stories can often create the best lives..

*(He did not tell that story.)*

# Storytelling

## Questions to Ask:

1. What story will you be telling in the future about the life you are living right now?

2. Can someone change their story? What steps does it take to make a change?

3. Who is sharing in your life story? What role are they playing?

4. What story can you tell about your past that has molded you into the person you are today?

## Variations

**Steve the Artist.** Frame the story by giving the group a main character of the story. Provide a background for the main character. "Steve the Artist was the happiest artist on the block but he had one secret he couldn't share…"

*(I could stare at you forever. That's not creepy, is it?)*

# Two Face

## Objective:

Draw EmojiCARDS quickly and have the students call out (or act out) the opposite emotion to develop an imaginative environment.

## Discovering Emotions:

1. Encourage the participants to gather in a circle. Circles are a favorite shape of the EmojiCARDS.

2. Instruct the group to think about the reactions they would have in certain scenarios. Then ask them to create the opposite reaction to that scenario...the absolute last emotion they would show in that situation.

3. Draw a card from the deck and invite everyone to mimic the emotion shown on the EmojiCARD. When you say, "Two Face!" the participants will mimic the opposite emotion.

4. Repeat with different EmojiCARDS. Ask the group to come up with different scenarios that would evoke emotion and then display the appropriate and opposite emotions.

*(Who ate my cookie?)*

# Two Face

## Processing Emotions:

It is not unusual for us to act one way but feel the opposite. It is not unusual for the people around us to act a certain way even though we know they don't feel that way. How do we handle these interactions? How do we match the emotions we feel with the actions we show?

## Questions to Ask:

1.  Have you ever been around someone who acted a certain way but proved different?

2.  Are there any areas of your life where you act one way but feel the opposite?

3.  What do you do when you find someone who is two-faced?

4.  What steps can you take to act the same on the outside as you feel on the inside?

## Variations

**Two Face Face Off.** Two-Face can is loads of fun in a group, but it is a blast as a competition between pairs. Ask the partners to pace off Old West style and quickly turn to show the opposite reaction. Fastest to show the opposite wins! Play best of three or just play for fun.

*(If anyone needs to play Two Face...it is me.)*

# List of Emotions

| | | |
|---|---|---|
| Admiring | Affection | Afraid |
| Agony | Aggressive | Amazement |
| Amusement | Anger | Anguish |
| Annoyed | Anxious | Apprehensive |
| Assertive | Assured | Astonished |
| Attached | Awe-Struck | Beleaguered |
| Bewitched | Bitter | Blissful |
| Bored | Calm | Capricious |
| Caring | Cautious | Charmed |
| Cheerful | Compassionate | Complacent |
| Compliant | Composed | Conceited |
| Concerned | Content | Crabby |
| Crazy | Cruel | Defeated |
| Defiant | Delighted | Dependent |
| Depressed | Disappointed | Disenchanted |
| Disgusted | Disillusioned | Distressed |
| Dreadful | Eager | Earnest |
| Easy-Going | Ecstatic | Elated |
| Embarrassed | Emotional | Enamored |
| Enchanted | Enraged | Enraptured |
| Enthralled | Enthusiastic | Envious |
| Euphoric | Exasperated | Excited |
| Exhausted | Extroverted | Exuberant |
| Fascinated | Fearful | Ferocious |
| Flummoxed | Flustered | Frightened |
| Frightful | Frustrated | Furious |
| Generous | Gloomy | Greedy |
| Grim | Grouchy | Grumpy |
| Guilty | Happy | Homesick |
| Hopeless | Horrified | Hostile |
| Humiliated | Hurt | Infatuated |
| Insecure | Insulted | Interested |
| Introverted | Irritated | Isolated |
| Jaded | Jealous | Jittery |
| Jolly | Jovial | Joyful |

# List of Emotions

| | | |
|---|---|---|
| Keen | Kind | Kindhearted |
| Laid-Back | Lazy | Loathing |
| Lonely | Longing | Lonely |
| Lulled | Lustful | Mad |
| Merry | Miserable | Modest |
| Mortified | Naughty | Needy |
| Neglected | Nervous | Open |
| Optimistic | Ornery | Outgoing |
| Outraged | Panicked | Passionate |
| Passive | Peaceful | Pensive |
| Pitiful | Placid | Pleased |
| Prideful | Proud | Pushy |
| Quarrelsome | Queasy | Quiet |
| Quirky | Rejected | Relieved |
| Remorseful | Resentful | Resigned |
| Revulsed | Roused | Sad |
| Sarcastic | Sardonic | Satisfied |
| Scared | Scornful | Self-Assured |
| Sentimental | Serene | Shameful |
| Shocked | Smug | Sorrowful |
| Sorry | Spellbound | Spiteful |
| Stingy | Stoic | Stressed |
| Subdued | Suffering | Surprised |
| Sympathetic | Tender | Tense |
| Terrified | Threatened | Thrilled |
| Timid | Tormented | Tranquil |
| Triumphant | Trusting | Uncomfortable |
| Unhappy | Upset | Vain |
| Vengeful | Vexed | Vigilant |
| Vivacious | Wacky | Warm |
| Weak | Wealthy | Weary |
| Weepy | Weird | Whimsical |
| Whiny | Wicked | Wild |
| Willing | Wise | Withdrawn |
| Woeful | Worthless | Wretched |

# Camps

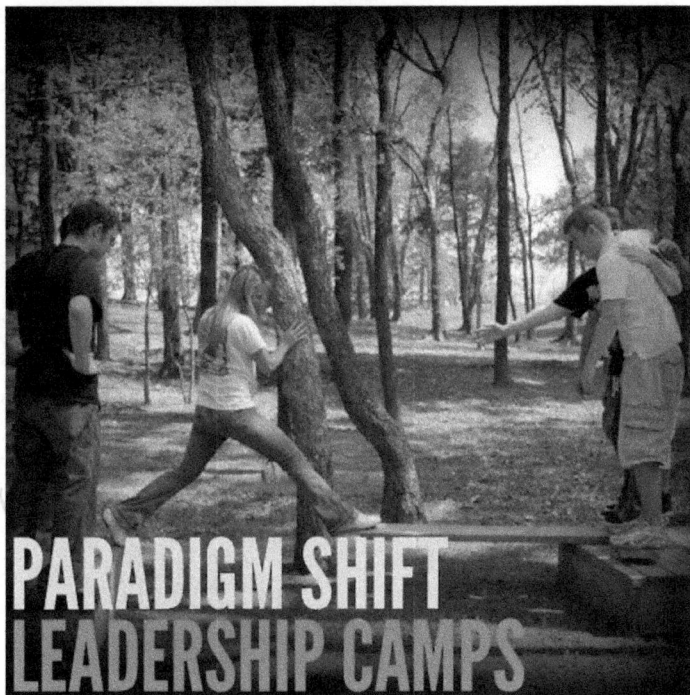

PARADIGM SHIFT LEADERSHIP CAMPS

Paradigm Shift will change the way you do camps. An exciting trend for educational and faith-based organizations is hosting a leadership camp for students. These camps incorporate a variety of aspects of your program, and have drastically increased student engagement.

Camps can be 1-5 days and held during summer break, spring break, or even a weekend. Paradigm Shift specializes in designing every aspect of these incredible camps. Each camp will be focused on your program's objectives and desires.

# Workshops

Each workshop is custom designed to work with your program's desired goals in mind. All workshops incorporate experiential learning (learning through a reflection of doing) and provide groups of all experience levels opportunities to create and enhance their leadership skills.

Our leadership workshops focus on strengths-based learning to cultivate powerful results. The Paradigm Shift staff creates every workshop based on your current curriculum, props and staff to develop an individualized event perfect your program!

# Keynotes

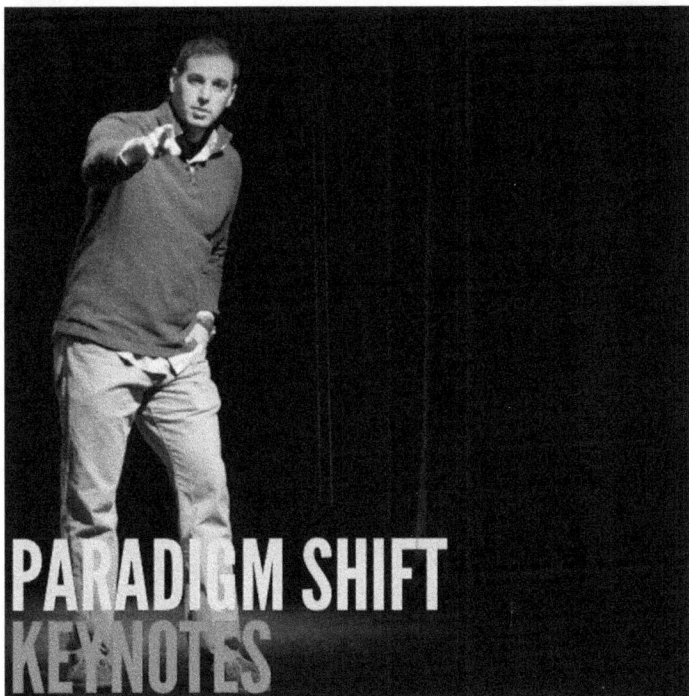

PARADIGM SHIFT
KEYNOTES

The Paradigm Shift team treats their keynotes as more than a lecture. It is a conversation. It is powerful. It is fun. More than anything, it is an opportunity for the audience to become engaged in the leadership material they are learning and to make it applicable to their own lives.

We use cutting edge theories and techniques from experiential-based learning to infuse leadership into every single one of our keynote addresses. We invite the audience to join us on an adventure of learning in a fresh and challenging way.

# Coaching

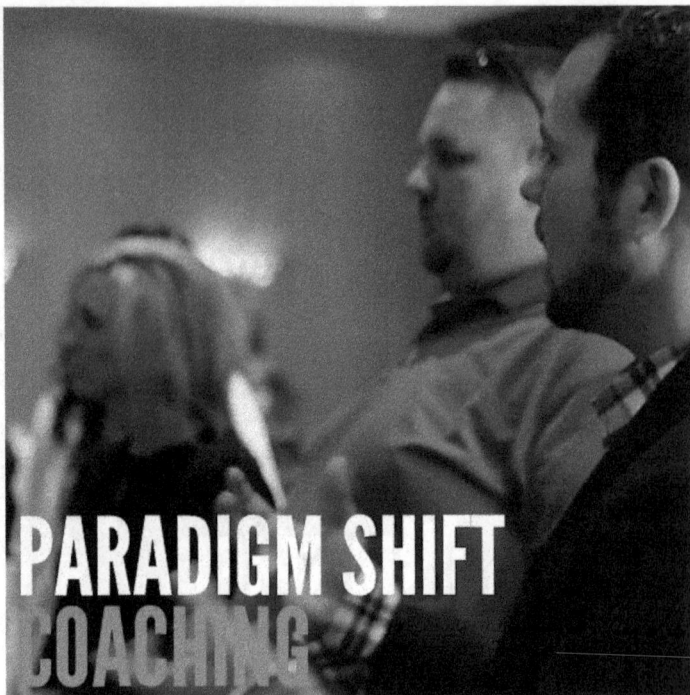

Would you like individual advice and coaching on how to lead your groups? Paradigm Shift offers individual consulting for trainers who want to take the next step in their facilitation.

Each participant enrolled in the coaching classes will also be involved in an online mastermind group that includes many of the best trainers from around the world. We will look at your programming to fine-tune your skills, update your curriculum, & provide you with individualized opportunities for leadership development.

# Train the Trainer

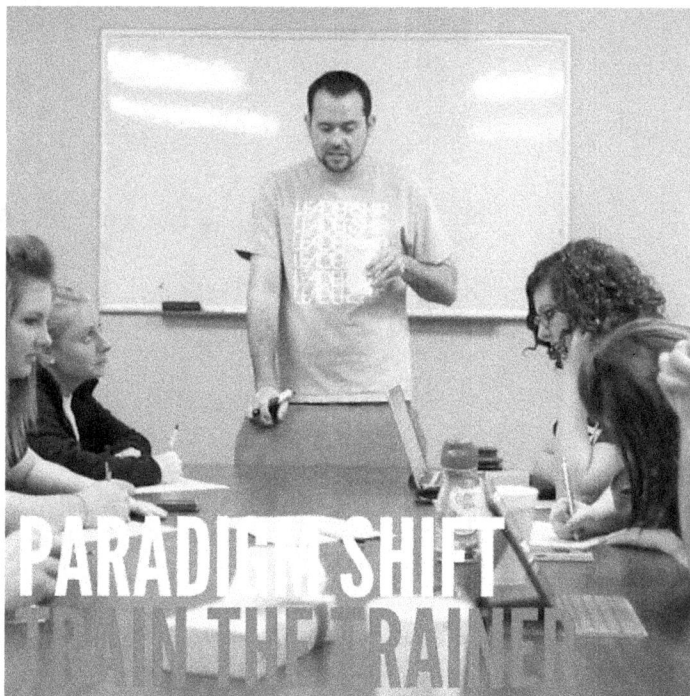

Paradigm Shift specializes in training group leaders who want to make a better connections with their participants. In these specialized trainings, our facilitators will walk you through the steps necessary to create better engagement, promote more powerful relationships, and allow substantial change to occur with a group.

Our curriculum has been proven through years of experience with thousands of groups. We follow the "Pool Party Process," a model that prepares groups to experience incredible learning and develop a call to action. These trainings are interactive, engaging, and completely customizable to your curriculum.

# EmojiCARDS

The activities in this book take full advantage of the fun, yet powerful emotions that are displayed on EmojiCARDS and EmojiCARDS 2! Group leaders of all skill levels and experiences can use EmojiCARDS to promote two separate areas of learning...discovering and processing emotions.

A pack of EmojiCARDS cost $15.

You can order EmojiCARDS for your group on the Paradigm Shift website:

www.myparadigmshift.org/store

## Paradigm Shift

Paradigm Shift offers leadership training and development with a primary focus to create opportunities for leaders to lead intentionally.

The Paradigm Shift consultants use practical leadership & adventure-based models to help leaders develop powerful relationships, set SMART goals, create personal responsibility, and develop a defined purpose.

We invite our participants to learn through dynamic keynotes, interactive workshops, online coaching, and customized training. Most importantly, Paradigm Shift will challenge your team to develop into leaders.

Find Paradigm Shift online at :

www.myparadigmshift.org

# The Authors

## Ryan Eller

Ryan is the founder and lead consultant of Paradigm Shift, which provides custom-built team-building and leadership training. Ryan has facilitated in 30 US states and hosted leadership conferences in Cuba, Brazil, and Australia. Ryan has the goal of hosting a leadership training in all 50 states and all 7 continents.

Ryan received his Bachelor's Degree in Mass Communication and Master's Degree in Higher Education Administration from NSU. He loves nothing more than a great Nick Collison screen while eating brinner with his beautiful wife Kristin and his little princess Jane.

## Jerrod Murr

Murr has been speaking to groups since he was 14. He really stepped up his game in his early twenties. Murr works with small groups in experiential learning settings, as well as keynotes to groups in the thousands. A few speaking highlights include the privilege of planning a leadership conference for over 300 pastors in Cuba, speaking to over 1,000 students in Brazil, and holding the microphone for his kindergarten class song.

Murr currently serves as the Director of 20 Camps and Leadership Develop for Paradigm Shift. He resides in Muskogee, OK with his wife, Jenn, daughter Adelae, and Josalyn. His favorite book is The Giving Tree, and he loves basketball, the OKC Thunder, and good coffee.

# Notes

# Notes

# Notes

# Notes

www.ingramcontent.com/pod-product-compliance
Lightning Source LLC
Chambersburg PA
CBHW071242090426
42736CB00014B/3184